Librarians like Leela help with all
They can:

- help students get ready for the
- help writers find important information for their books
- help customers find the perfect book to read.

Whatever you need at the library, a librarian will be able to help.

Joining the library

It does not cost any money to join a public library. Anyone can use the books and equipment there. Once you have joined the library, you can borrow books to take home and read.

Leela loves welcoming new members, recommending books and helping people find exactly what they need.

Leela the Librarian

by Smriti Prasadam-Halls
Illustrated by Ana Sebastián

Contents

OXFORD
UNIVERSITY PRESS

Meet Leela!

Leela

> Hello! Welcome to the library!

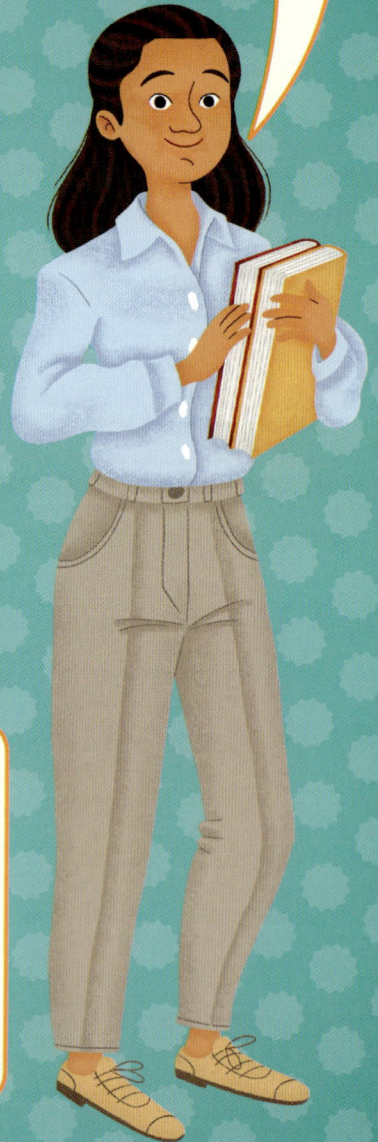

Leela is a librarian.

She works at a public library. Leela helps people find information about anything and everything they need to know.

Looking for a book

Leela can search the computer to see if a book you want is in stock. If it isn't, she may be able to order it from another library.

If someone else is already borrowing the book, Leela can reserve it for you. That means you can borrow the book as soon as it is returned.

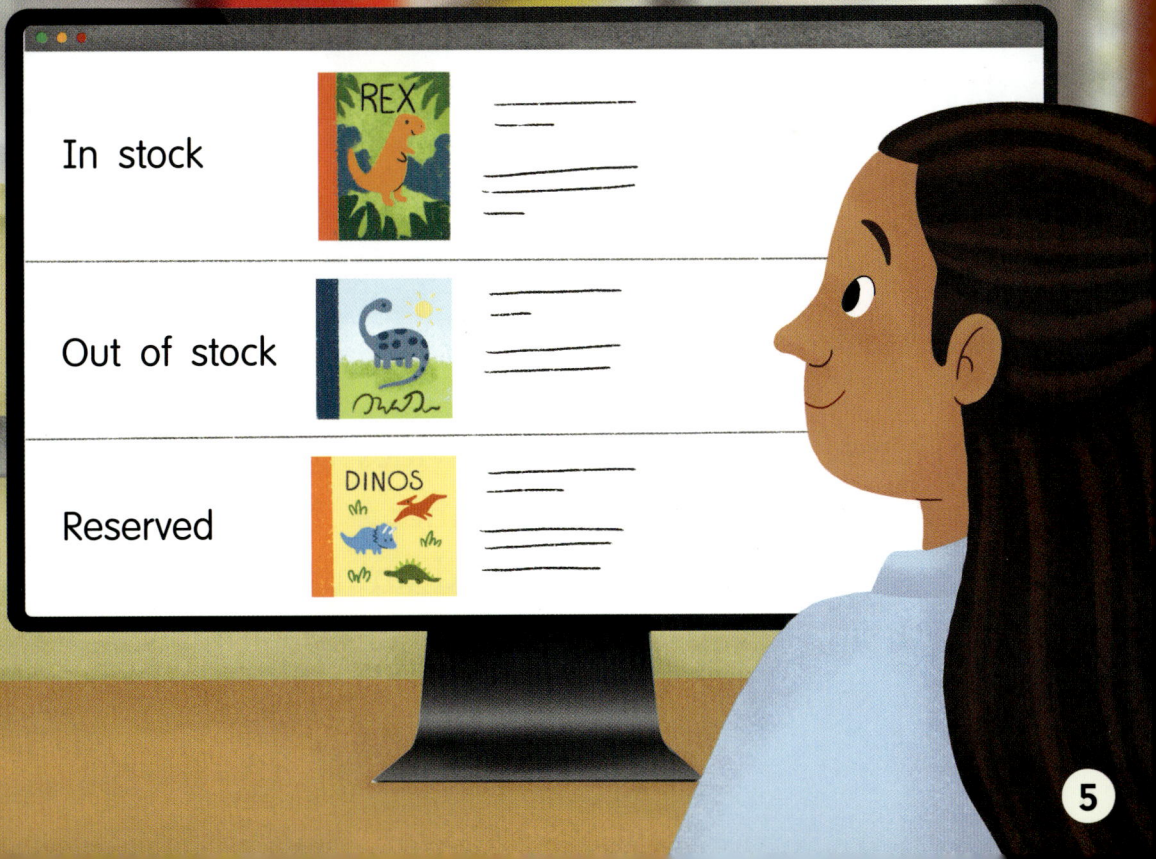

In stock

Out of stock

Reserved

How do librarians know exactly where to find information and books?

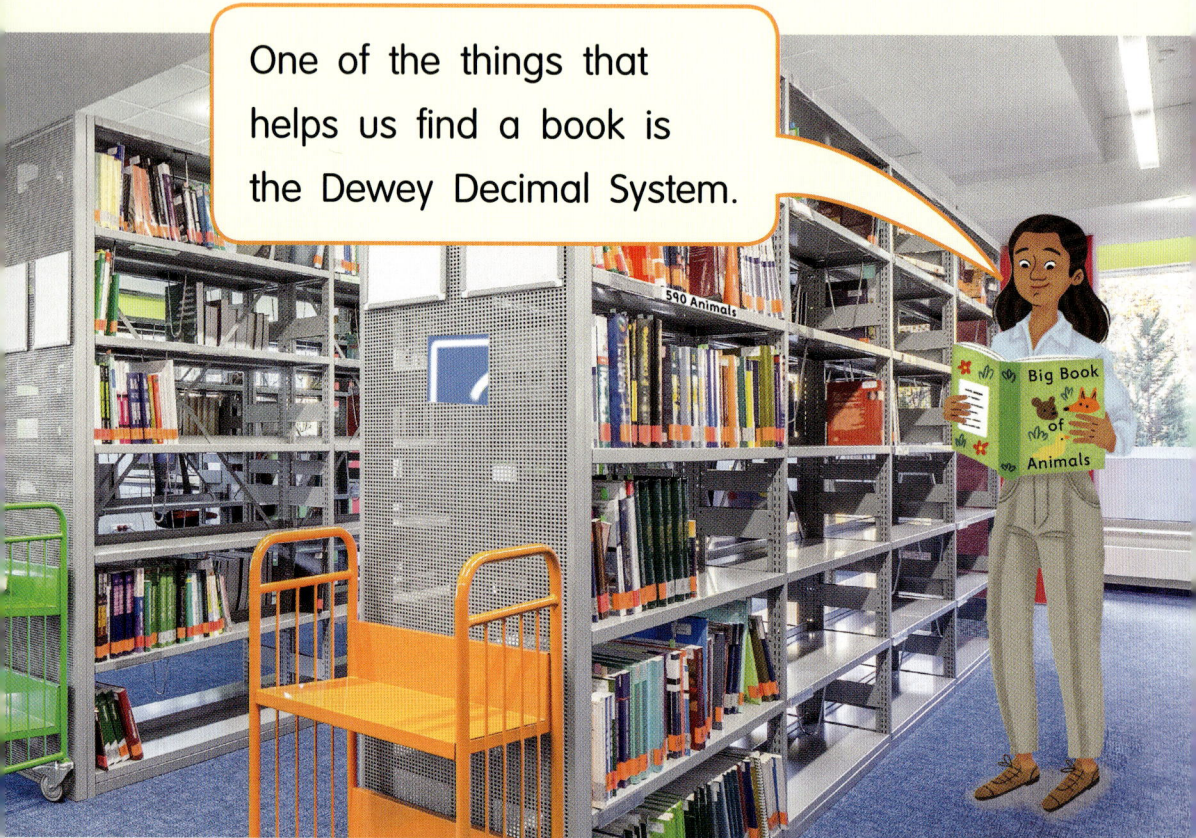

One of the things that helps us find a book is the Dewey Decimal System.

The Dewey Decimal System divides books by subject. Each subject has a special number – for example, books about plants are 580 and animal books are 590. So, if you want a book about animals, find the shelf with number 590!

No matter what book you are looking for, there will be a special number for it. A librarian will be able to help you find it.

Could you help me find a book about cooking?

Yes! Cooking is number 641. We can find all the cookery books over here!

The first libraries

Leela enjoys reading about the earliest libraries.

The earliest known library was discovered in Iraq. It belonged to a king who lived more than 2500 years ago!

Instead of books, the library had more than 30000 clay tablets. The tablets were covered in ancient writing called cuneiform (*say*: cue-na-form).

The most famous ancient library was the Library of Alexandria in Egypt. The books there would have been written on **papyrus** scrolls. The library was destroyed in a war more than 2000 years ago. Many important books were lost forever.

One ancient library is still in use today! It was set up in Morocco more than 1000 years ago.

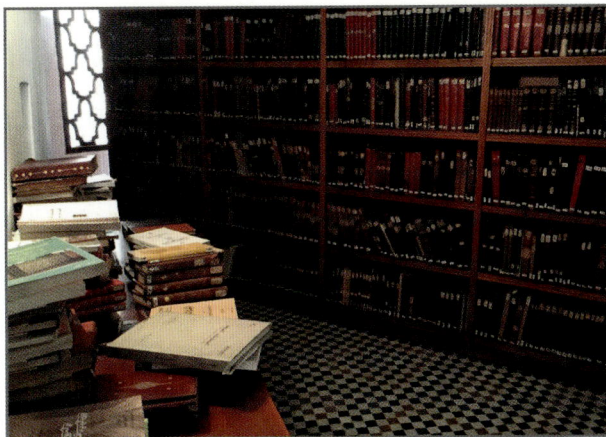

Events

At her library, Leela runs many events. There is always lots going on.

Book groups meet to talk about the books they are reading. Readers discuss their favourite parts of the story.

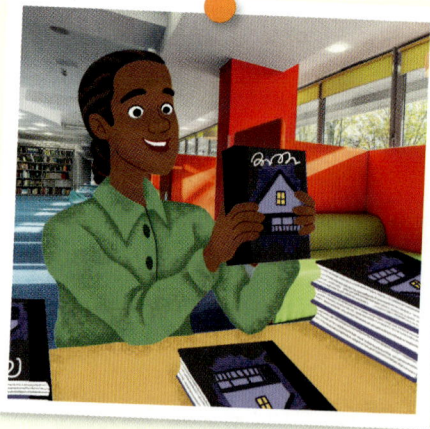

Sometimes authors and illustrators give talks about their books. People ask them questions and find out what it is like to make books.

Leela welcomes people of all ages to the library. She helps run courses to help people learn how to use technology – like computers, mobile phones and tablets. She shows people how to use the internet to find out more about things that interest them.

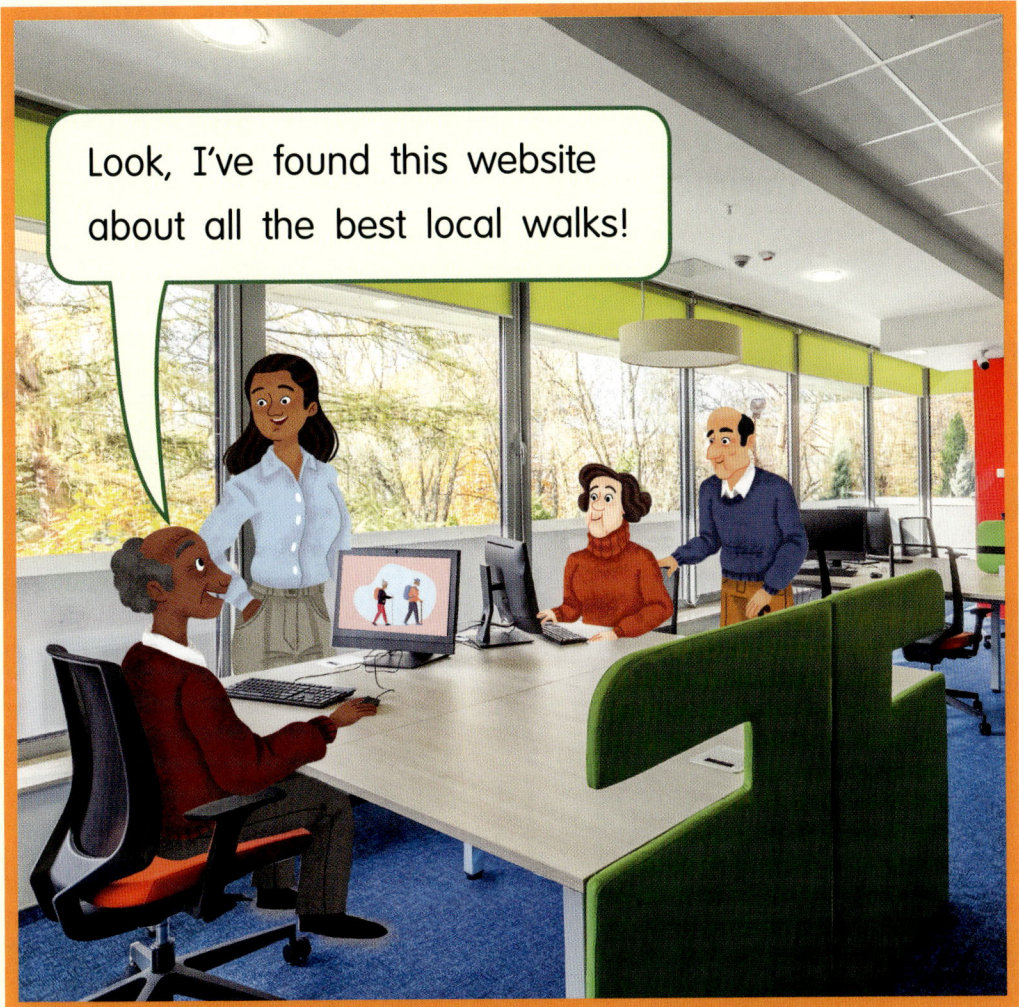

Look, I've found this website about all the best local walks!

Story time

The library is fun for children, too. Leela runs activities to get children interested in words and pictures from when they are tiny.

Babies, toddlers and their carers love going along to special story times. There are stories to listen to, actions and rhymes to join in with, and songs to sing. Sometimes there are drawing and colouring activities, too.

The story times are a great way to get very young children interested in reading. This will make it easier for them to learn to read when they are older. It also helps families to connect and have fun together. Babies love looking at picture books and listening to stories.

All sorts of libraries

Leela works at the public library, which is open to everyone. But there are lots of other specialist libraries, at places like universities, museums and hospitals. Some schools have libraries, too!

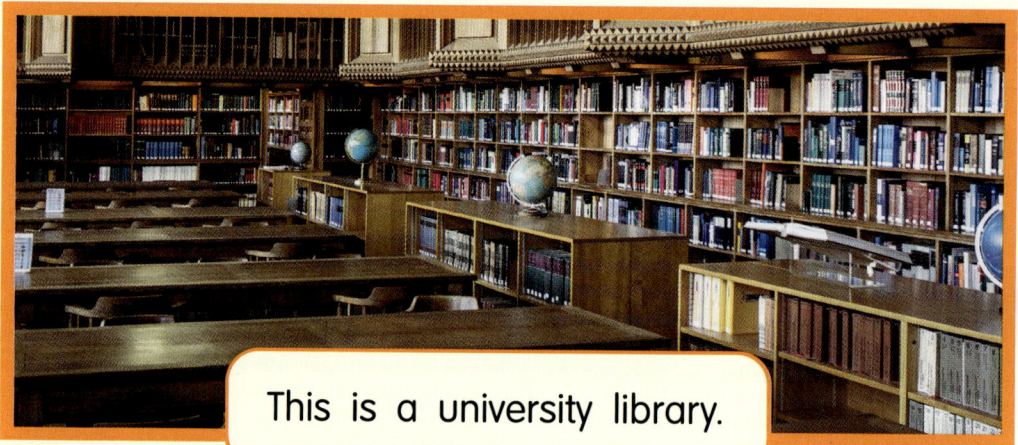

This is a university library.

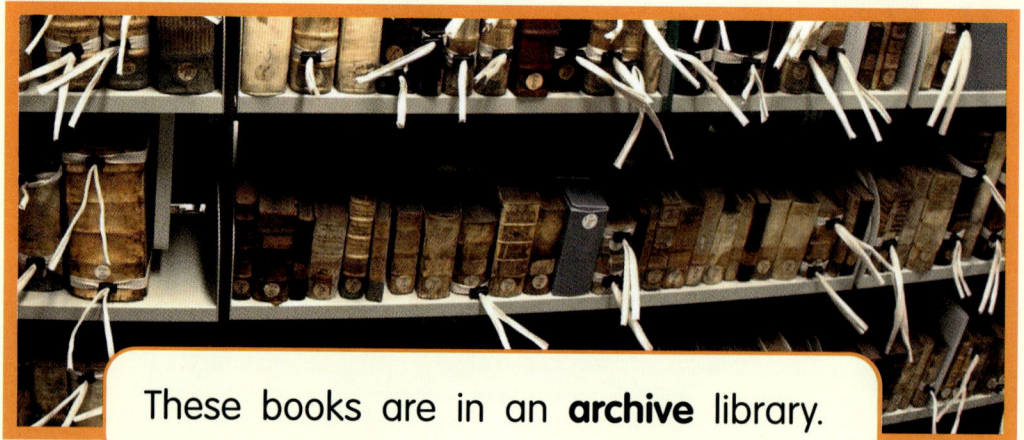

These books are in an **archive** library.

Helping at my school library inspired me to become a librarian! I kept the shelves tidy and arranged book displays. I liked seeing which books were the most popular!

If you are lucky, you may have a librarian at your school. They can help you pick out great books and help you with projects while you are at school.

Little libraries

Leela sometimes helps children with projects. Milly has to **research** libraries for school and asks Leela for help finding information.

Libraries come in all shapes and sizes. Tiny libraries are popping up in all sorts of curious and unusual places. There, people can swap books. Bring a book you've already read and swap it for a different book!

Leela helps Milly research on the internet. Look at all the places where little libraries have appeared:

in the woods

www.littlelibraries.com X

Little Libraries

at the beach

BEACH LIBRARY

LITTLE FREE LIBRARY
TAKE ONE   LEAVE ONE

in a bird box

in a phone box

Could you turn something into a little library at your school?

Mobile libraries

It is more difficult to get to a library when you do not live in a town or city.

Wow, some libraries bring the books to your house!

Mobile libraries visit many villages in the countryside. These libraries are usually special vans, with shelves full of books to borrow.

Some travelling libraries can reach areas that are even more remote.

The Biblioburro

There is a donkey mobile library in Colombia. Two donkeys called Alfa and Beto carry children's books in their saddle bags.

The Camel Mobile Library

Camels in Kenya travel through the desert, carrying books to travelling communities.

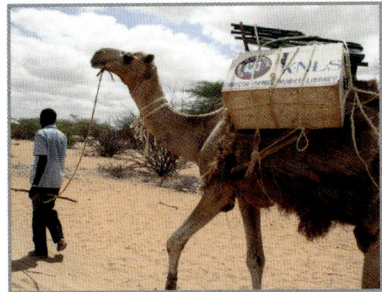

Boat libraries

In Sweden and Norway, lots of people live on tiny islands. Boat libraries bring books to them!

Leela's library

Leela loves being a librarian.

I like meeting all the different people who come in. There's such a lovely atmosphere in the library. The library is an important part of the community.

Many people want to browse or study, but some visitors just want to come in for a friendly chat.

Librarians do not just look after books. Leela's library also has:

- a section full of films that you can borrow
- a section full of books in **Braille**
- monthly magazines and **journals**
- daily newspapers
- audiobooks to borrow and listen to.

I love the audiobook section! It's great to listen to an audiobook on a long car journey.

Could you be a librarian?

You might like to be a librarian if you enjoy:

- helping people
- finding out about the latest books, films, music and magazines
- working with computers
- knowing lots of information and how to find more
- searching for answers to tricky questions
- organizing things
- problem solving
- planning exciting events
- giving information
- reading.

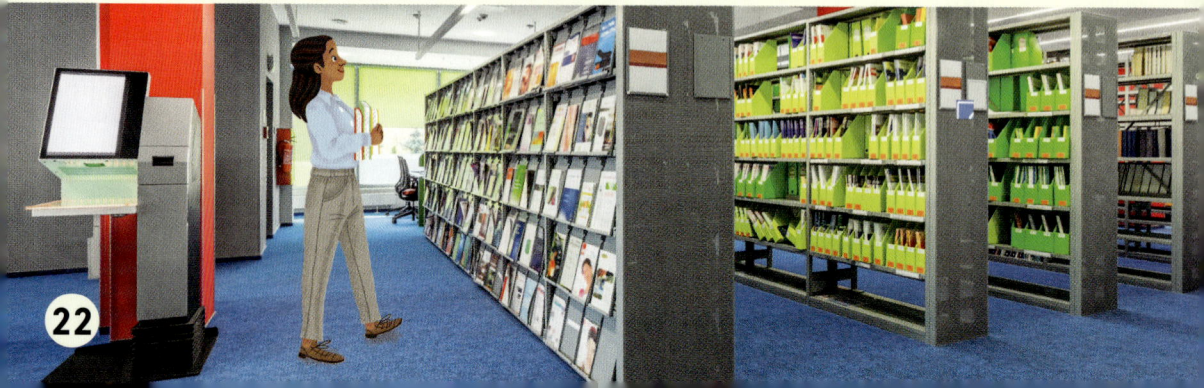

These are just some of the interests and skills needed to be a good librarian. If you think you would enjoy some of this, then you might like to become a librarian one day!

And if you have not visited your local library yet, today could be the perfect day to go along and join.

I hope to see you soon!

Glossary

archive: a place that stores historical documents

Braille: a system of raised dots that are read by feeling with the fingertips

journals: special types of magazine

papyrus: a kind of paper made from the stems of reeds, used in ancient Egypt

research: find out information about something

Index